Billie Jean King

Jennifer Strand

abdopublishing.com

Published by Abdo Zoom™, PO Box 398166, Minneapolis, Minnesota 55439. Copyright © 2017 by Abdo Consulting Group, Inc. International copyrights reserved in all countries. No part of this book may be reproduced in any form without written permission from the publisher. Abdo Zoom™ is a trademark and logo of Abdo Consulting Group, Inc.

Printed in the United States of America, North Mankato, Minnesota
072016
092016

Cover Photo: Universal/TempSport/Corbis
Interior Photos: Universal/TempSport/Corbis, 1; Bettmann/Getty Images, 4, 17; Lennox Mclendon/AP Images, 5; Jim Pringle/AP Images, 6–7; AP Images, 9, 12, 14, 15; Ray Stubblebine/AP Images, 10; Anthony Camerano/AP Images, 11; Stephen Chernin/AP Images, 18; Manuel Balce Ceneta/AP Images, 19

Editor: Brienna Rossiter
Series Designer: Madeline Berger
Art Direction: Dorothy Toth

Publisher's Cataloging-in-Publication Data
Names: Strand, Jennifer, author.
Title: Billie Jean King / by Jennifer Strand.
Description: Minneapolis, MN : Abdo Zoom, [2017] | Series: Trailblazing athletes
    | Includes bibliographical references and index.
Identifiers: LCCN 2016941528 | ISBN 9781680792508 (lib. bdg.) |
    ISBN 9781680794182 (ebook) | 9781680795073 (Read-to-me ebook)
Subjects: LCSH: King, Billie Jean--Juvenile literature. | Tennis players--United
    States--Biography--Juvenile literature. | Women tennis players--United
    States--Biography--Juvenile literature.
Classification: DDC 796.342092 [B]--dc23
LC record available at http://lccn.loc.gov/2016941528

Table of Contents

Introduction

Billie Jean King was
a star tennis player.

She is also an **activist**.
She works to help
women in sports.

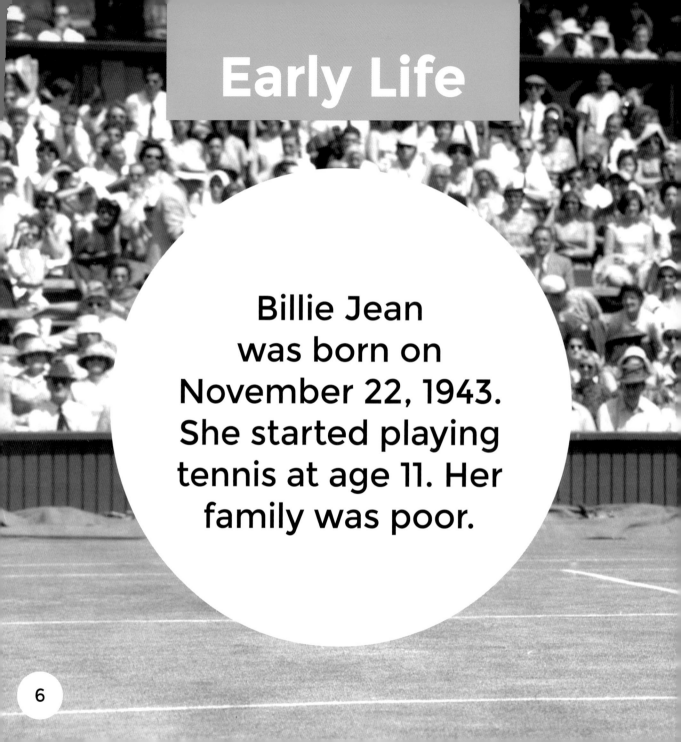

Billie Jean was born on November 22, 1943. She started playing tennis at age 11. Her family was poor.

But she worked hard.

Leader

King became a great tennis player.
She was known for her speed.
In 1966 she won Wimbledon.

It is one of the most important tennis tournaments.

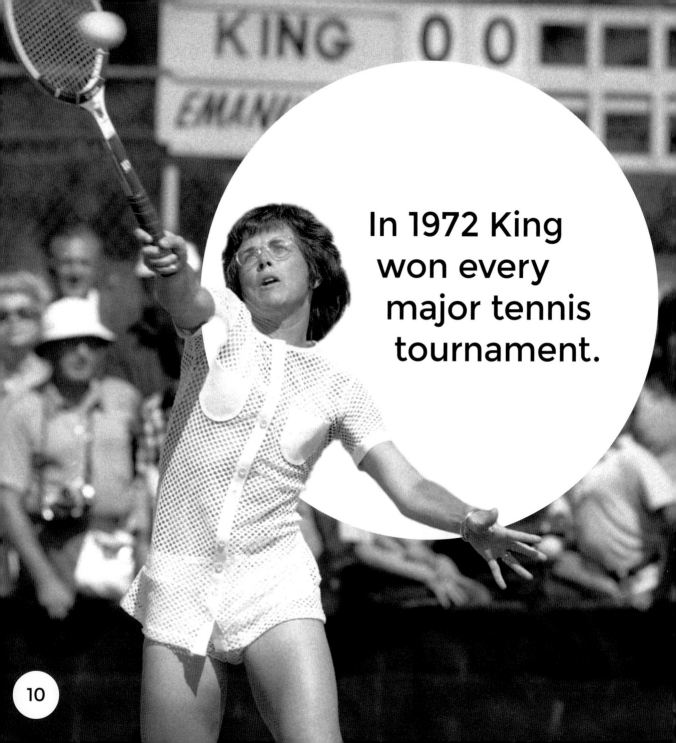

In 1972 King won every major tennis tournament.

She was the world's top
women's tennis player.

King was
a star.

But women **athletes** were paid less than men. King thought this was unfair. She worked to change it.

She played against a men's tennis champion. It was a huge event.

King won. She showed that women were serious athletes, too.

Legacy

King has long worked for **social change**. She supported a law called Title IX. It gives female athletes in schools equal **funding** to males.

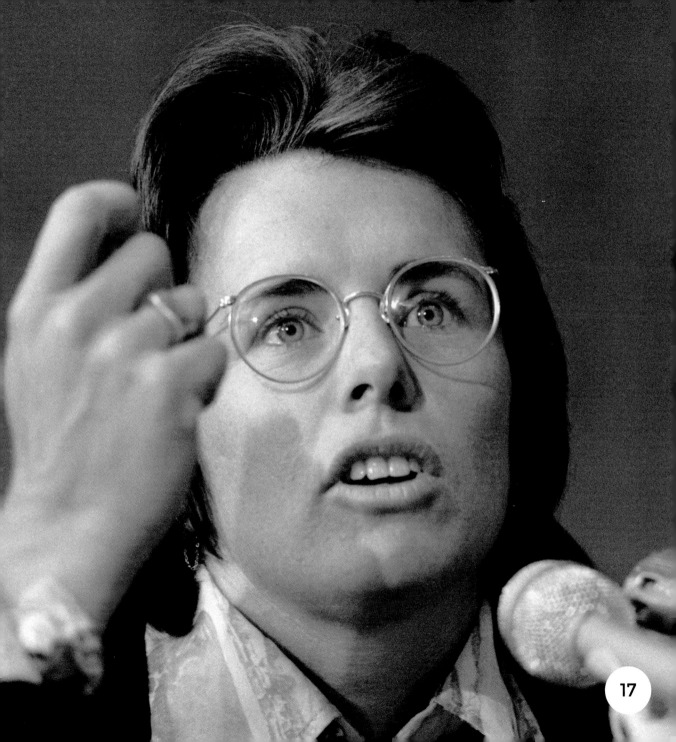

King's work helps more girls play sports.

She still works to help all people have equal **rights**.

Billie Jean King

Born: November 22, 1943

Birthplace: Long Beach, California

Sport: Tennis

Known For: King was a tennis champion. She is still a women's rights activist.

 Key Dates

1943: Billie Jean Moffitt is born on November 22.

1961: Billie Jean wins her first Wimbledon title.

1965: Billie Jean and Larry King marry. They later divorce.

1972: Billie Jean King works to help Title IX be passed.

1973: King beats men's tennis champion Bobby Riggs on September 20.

1987: King is elected to the International Tennis Hall of Fame.

Glossary

activist - a person who works for change.

athlete - a person who plays a sport.

funding - money that is given or used for a special purpose, such as to make something happen.

rights - the things that people can do under the law.

social change - a change in the way people in a community think, act, or treat each other.

Booklinks

For more information
on Billie Jean King, please visit
booklinks.abdopublishing.com

Z**m In on Biographies!

Learn even more with the Abdo Zoom
Biographies database. Check out
abdozoom.com for more information.

Index